Against the Woods' Dark Trunks

MERCER UNIVERSITY PRESS

Endowed by

TOM WATSON BROWN
and
THE WATSON-BROWN FOUNDATION, INC.

Against the Woods' Dark Trunks

POEMS

Jack B. Bedell

MERCER UNIVERSITY PRESS
Macon, Georgia

MUP/ P650

© 2022 by Mercer University Press
Published by Mercer University Press
1501 Mercer University Drive
Macon, Georgia 31207

26 25 24 23 22   5 4 3 2 1

Books published by Mercer University Press are printed on acid-free paper that
meets the requirements of the American National Standard for Information
Sciences—Permanence of Paper for Printed Library Materials.

Printed and bound in the United States.

This book is set in Adobe Garamond Pro.

Cover/jacket design by Burt&Burt.
Cover art by and courtesy of Alanna Sparanese, www.alannasparanese.com.

ISBN   978-0-88146-856-4
Cataloging-in-Publication Data is available from the Library of Congress

CONTENTS

ACKNOWLEDGMENTS

"Yes, Yes We Do," *8 Poems*; "Présage," *About Place*; *City of Nature,* and "In the Open Space of a Crawfish Pond," *Anthropocene*; "Sometimes the Alligator Gets to Write the Ending," *Backstory*; "Owl- and Wolf-Infested Lands," *Barren*; *Window with Ladder—Too Late to Help, Black Bough Poetry*; "Gougou," *Breadcrumbs*; "Conflation," *Burning House*; "Neighbor Tones," *The Cabinet of Heed*; "Mil Máscaras," *Cotton Xenomorph*; "P.V. O'Neill's Grave," *Dark Marrow*; "Until the Rice Boils Over," *Delta Poetry Review*; "Amano," *EcoTheo Review*; "Sometimes You Get the Bull, Sometimes," *Elephants Never*; "Iapetus," *Fresh Air Poetry*; "Wendigo," *Gingerbread House*; "Augury," *Glass: A Journal of Poetry*; "Another Night, Just," *The Hopper*; "Marsh Horses," "Rolled Over into Waves," and "Traiteuse," *isacoustic*; "La Lechuza," *Juke Joint Magazine*; "Grassman" and "St. Lucy Led to Her Martyrdom," *L'Ephemere*; "New Beach, Elmer's Island," "Six More Weeks," and "The White Alligator," *Middle House Review*; "All Spirit Must Take a Name" and "The News, Again," *Mineral Lit*; "La Llorona Rests Her Feet in the Creek," *Moonchild Magazine*; "Stink," *The Night Heron Barks*; "Pecan Grove with Body Farm," *Okay Donkey*; "Dusk, Meditation," *One*; "Goujon," *Oxidant | Engine*; "There Is Wind," *Parentheses Journal*; "Just Another Day in November" and "Like Asin at the Edge of the Woods," *Pidgeonholes*; "Memory: Bats," *Porridge*; "The Pale Man's Eyes Never Leave the Horizon" and "Q&A," *Rhythm & Bones*; "Death Comes to the Banquet Table," *Riggwelter Journal*; "Beached Whale, Terrebonne Parish, 2016," *Rust + Moth*; "Black Rush," *San Pedro River Review*; *Serpents and Insects, 1647, The Shore*; "Burn, Hollywood, Burn," *Southern Quarterly*; "Littoral," *Speak the Magazine*; "Three Steps Off the Ropes" and "Memory: Unsorted," *Sport Literate*; "Memory: Touch," *Trampset*; "Bill Evans on *Kind of Blue*," *Twist in Time*; "Voucher," *UCity Review*; "Disparition," *Whale Road Review*; "There Is No Train But the Tracks Will Take You There," *Yes Poetry*.

"Of Proxies and Moonshadow" appeared in the Slender Man anthology, *Mansion* (Dancing Girl Press 2019). "Beached Whale, Terrebonne Parish, 2016" appeared in *Rewilding: Poems for the Environment* (Flexible Press, 2020).

Another Night, Just

Our day starts with news
      of another mass shooting out West.

We learn about bump stocks,
      rush to get things ready for the ride to school,

exams, football games. The rest rolls downhill fast
      until I'm on my belly in a gas station parking lot

crawling over gravel to place a jack
      under the axle of my truck, right next

to a blown-out sidewall. My daughter's crouched over
      asking me if I know what *deposition* is.

"Not like in court," she says, "like when big rocks
      break into small chunks of stuff."

There's a cricket with me under the truck, somewhere,
      and it answers with a quick *scree* before I can.

My son's head pokes under the door
      on the other side, and he tells us

that if we slowed down a recording of a field full of crickets
      it would sound just like a choir of people

singing in perfect harmony. And even right there
      lying on the ground, rocks cutting into my stomach,

I have to laugh at how easily "if" and "just"
      roll off his tongue.

Until the Rice Boils Over

If I could have her make one more meal,
sweat onions and celery in a buttered skillet—

roast seared on all sides and set aside on a plate,
flour browning in the hot pan for gravy, her hands
busy like bumble bees over azaleas.
                                                            Sunlight
would turn the kitchen counters honey-gold,
and all clanks would make song.
                                                            I'd stand
as close to her as I could without getting in the way,
not a clumsy child just wanting one taste,
                                                            but
a parent myself, willing to wait my turn
until the children are done running the yard
and the dog has gone to ground under the bushes.

The waiting would be enough, no need
to hurry the fire under the rice.

Yes, Yes We Do

What type of person chases
      down the snake that's just
          bitten him on the ankle?

His anger must be pure,
      clean-burning fuel, rich
enough to give him speed
      to run down the serpent's tail,
snatch it up by writhing curves
      and chomp off its head
with his own teeth.

The metallic taste of snake's blood
      must surely dance on his tongue
          like the sweet dervish of revenge.

And don't we all deserve to feel
      that kind of surge just once?

The pleasant denouement
      of the snake's head spat out
          plunking onto the dirt path, too?

Bill Evans on *Kind of Blue*

The melody off Evans' keys
      grows underneath the horns
like a python in a Florida marsh,
         the notes easy to catch,
all prey without trees to climb.
      His hands feed in the horns'
shadows. Cymbals and snare
        scurry away as he slides
through these tunes. Reeds
      take flight any time his line
flicks near their feet. And always
        the glow of the trumpet
rains down on everything
      in warm bursts, sometimes
a bath, sometimes a wave
        covering miles of undergrowth
in its smooth wail, its long dawn, while
      this hunt below just glides along.

Mil Máscaras

My sons ask me
                to put on the blue mask
                    with the white leather
phoenix stretched across its eye holes.
As soon as I tighten the laces
      I am Mil Máscaras,
                    a man with a thousand
holds in my arsenal. I do not need
          a partner to face down their tag team,
only a constant glide
                  from suplex to boston crab
to standing test of strength
                    with fingers intertwined
and wrists cocked toward
       submission. No time for breath,
no mocking celebration, no
                      mercy.
Inside this circle, I am
          the people's champion, a bronze,
oiled tower of power. This is what my sons
       have called down upon themselves,
              the blue-eyed
                    bringer of pain
from parts unknown.

Iapetus

—for Robbie and Cathy Wallace

My daughter has slept all week
    with a tiny jar of salt
    under her pillow I brought back
from a trip to West Virginia.

I told her the salt's history,
    how it was mined from brine
    left there by an ancient ocean
trapped under the Appalachians,

waves way too old to have carried
    boats. She wants to dream
    of serpents' coils rolling
just under that water's surface,

giant, translucent scales
    floating around her bed.
    She would love to wake one day
with a new recipe for chocolate cake.

She'd sprinkle the batter with this salt
    before baking it, slice pieces
    of her dreams to share
with her brothers and me, adrift and all.

Amano

—Frank Relle Gallery, NOLA

Even what's left of this broken cypress tree
    hasn't given up reaching for the sky.

Busted dead center, and toppled over
    into the lake, its branches still climb

toward the stars bursting over this swamp.
    The sun has surrendered its sky, glowing

just under the horizon line, the lake's surface
    stilled to exhaustion absent any breeze.

Herons have tucked in for the night.
    This old tree, though, standing tip-toed

on its roots, just won't cede to the pull
    of water, the notion that all things

must go to ground patiently. As long
    as there is light somewhere, it's worth the reach.

All Spirit Must Take a Name

—Adams, Tennessee

Not the hate so much
      as a wounded heart, even
            the dim memory of hope,

can slide a chair across wooden floors,
      or stoke the dying embers
            in the bedroom fireplace

to burning flame. Meanness cannot
      slam doors. Only wishes
            gone cold can move anything,

anywhere. And what is a name
      if it isn't hope? Even if
            you were not Kate alive,

take that name to twist
      your scream into voice. Use it
            as an answer when they beg

to know who's poisoned John Bell.
      Let them cry that name
            into the mouths of caves

when their blood tells them
      they will not find love in a boy,
            will never shake the dark

as long as they know your name,
      will feel you in the murmurs
            every bed makes before dawn.

Six More Weeks

—Bonnet Carré Spillway, May 2019

Six more weeks of the spillway
      dumping freshwater into Lake Catherine,
and the bodies of dolphin and sea turtles
      are washing up on shore. Crabs
burrow deep into the lake's bottom.
      Oyster beds turn to dead shell.

With such a death grip
      on our land, guarding it against
the rising river, can we help
      but squeeze out ghosts?

Serpents and Insects, 1647

—oil on canvas, Otto Marseus van Schrieck,
New Orleans Museum of Art

White moths hover in spare light
  and snakes coil around mushrooms
    growing at the base of this tree.

All life must escape the darkness
  of these leaves to feed, or to fight.
    Even the blue trail of a fly

moves away from the leaves' black
  veins toward its own end. Everything
    close to the tree's trunk reduces

to textures, hiding places
  where fangs flash against each other
    and the darting tongues of frogs

spear wings straight out of the air.
  Ground hard rock, and sky gone
    dark—a single vine in memory of sun.

Gougou

—Gulf of Saint Lawrence

Feel her floating underneath the water's surface,
moving slowly enough to lift a boat
with her swell but leave no wake.

She pulls scales from her hips, frees them
to float in the water like manta rays.
She drags her huge feet through wreckage

strewn along the gulf bed, has no fear
of lightning, no need for the moon
to pull her toward pain. She could

eat a thousand men and not sit still,
her hunger flowing like wave.

Burn, Hollywood, Burn

My son's working on a diorama
     for his *Gone with the Wind* project.
The whole thing has to fit in a sideways shoebox,
     so his vision of Tara lit up by burning fields
can't make the cut. He settles on a scene
     with Clark Gable on one knee in the parlor
pitching an alternate future to Vivien Leigh.
     He finds a good shot of them online,
prints it out in living color, and glues it
     to drymount as a cutout. Same with a table
of fresh flowers, a set of curio shelves, a velvet arm chair.
     He snips out one side of the box for a picture window,
lines the inside edges with gold satin for drapes,
     but he can't find an image of a fiery field anywhere
to match his notion of what a burning legacy looks like.
     The forest fires out west come close, but give off
too much smoke. We mess with the saturation
     on a pic of the aurora borealis but can't get the shine
just right. I suggest some cane fields on fire,
     but he says that's way too "literal." How about
we Google *apology*, I ask, apply some Boolean range
     [Weinstein, Allen, Louis C. K.];
print a slough of those words out and tape them
     into the window hole? I'm sure that might figure
to add another dimension to this 3D universe.

Memory: Unsorted

My father liked to watch fights
    with his eyes closed.

He worked in his uncle's store
    as a child scraping color

off all the meat in the front cooler.
    When the shop closed on weekends,

the whole neighborhood showed up
    on the porch to listen to matches

on his uncle's giant Phillips.
    They'd all balled their fists

through Louis's revenge on Schmeling.
    He said it sounded like two minutes

of murder. He'd clenched his eyes
    and prayed for Louis through 12 rounds

of Billy Conn, thinking the whole time
    his uncle's porch was sinking.

Years after that old radio had died,
    he'd listen to the TV fights

from a side room, pacing. He thought
    Sonny Liston looked tired all the time,

but his fists sounded angry and his fights
    always lasted longer than Dad imagined

they could. When I got old enough to watch
        fights with him, I'd think he was napping

until the pop of Frazier's left hook
        or the earthquake of Foreman's body shots

would make him wince, then smile
        like a breeze had blown across his porch.

Wendigo

The real haunting is the light itself.
—Erica Wright

When you speak his name a second time,
    do not grin. His spirit will slip

past your teeth into your core. All light
    will wane from your eyes,

and shadows of horns will sprout
    from your shoulder blades.

As much as you would like to hear
    trees whisper, the moon cry,

it is not worth inviting him
    to reverse your blood's flow.

If you are lucky enough to spot him
    floating in the stranger's shadow

sitting next to you on the bus,
    beg the driver to let you off

before he smells how much you want.
    Take as many with you as will come.

Or at least remind them before you leave
    how right it is to fear the near at hand.

Disparition

With the house full of a screen door's slam,
     every shadow holds a scar. No more

shuffle of slipper across wood, no
     smell of onions sweating in a skillet,

burl of water running for a bath. Only
     breeze through open windows

and creaks from timber settling toward ground.
     Somewhere, starlings dervish against

a purple sky, a river cuts its way
     into stone. And past all that,

a spirit carries its own weight
     into the night's quiet embrace.

Grassman

He leaves a hole
            in the wheat

large enough for four deer
to sleep in close circle,

            their legs
tucked underneath their bodies
to treasure all warmth.

His smell still there, always,
            sticks thick to the grain

like disease armadillos spray.

You can wait for him
            in this space

if your heart can face
            such vacuum of time.

Sit down in his clearing.
Look up at his piece of sky.

Open yourself to absence
as August dirt misses rain.

Know that he will return,
            slipping into the field

like breath through lips,
his broad shoulders blotting out

            the moon's dull glow.

Of Proxies and Moonshadow

The way a stab wound smiles
    when the skin around it shifts,

how nineteen of those wounds sing
    like a choir when the girl

bleeds herself across the forest's floor
    towards highway whispers

and broken light. Then the slender shape
    pressed into the thinnest shadows

of trees. Not her guide or guardian,
    not a friend holding her hair

out of the blood soaking her jacket—
    hands have rent her

in his stead, have washed themselves
    with her innocence

to gain favor he would not grant.
    And what of this moon

makes it leave more darkness
    along the grass than glow?

P.V. O'Neill's Grave

—Oakland Cemetery, Shreveport, LA

An oak tree has left its ghost
    on this plot with crumbled
        marble and mangled wrought iron

bent all around the tombstone.
    The psalm engraved below
        O'Neill's name failed

to offer any peace against
    the weight of that trunk,
        calm breeze and cool water

or not. Today, the grass is cut tight
    at the site, and all the bits of stone
        have been stacked neatly

inside what remains of the fence.
    No roots left from the falling, though,
        and even fewer signs it matters.

Three Steps Off the Ropes

There are wrestlers that have died in the ring. And if you ask them
while they're alive if they would give their life in the ring,
they would say absolutely they would. —César Barrón (1968-2019)

That's all it took for Silver King to launch
        himself off the ropes into his opponent,
                one last flying clothesline, one final

shoulder, just enough breath left to drape an arm
        over Juventud's chest. The ref's count
        One, then Two, then

the slow hang of the ref's hand,
        the swell of the crowd,
            and—no matter how bright the lights

hanging from the arena's ceiling,
        how unholy late the kick-out—
        the script's end.

Just Another Day in November

—List Murder House, *Antieau Gallery, NOLA*

How ordinary would a house have to be
        to hold an entire family dead, zipped up
                in sleeping bags on the living room floor

for a solid month before any of the neighbors,
        or teachers, or police thought to ask?
                And what would the soccer moms

who sat next to John List on the sidelines
        of his son's final game, or the bank tellers
                who closed out all of his accounts that afternoon,

say if you told them List spent the end of that day
        scrubbing drag marks from the kitchen tiles
                and cutting his own face out of family photos?

To look at this house, even the next morning,
        it would be hard to admit that kind of evil
                exists in this world. Not with Wonder Bread

left open on the counter, or fresh ham in the fridge,
        or church music playing softly on the radio.
                Not in the fall with the leaves just starting to turn.

Window with Ladder—Too Late to Help

—Leandro Erich, 2006
New Orleans Museum of Art

So few steps on this ladder to lead
us nowhere. So little time to help
anything before the weight of Lateness
swings on the end of a chain
to knock away all brick around this window.

The opening remains, though,
and fresh air flows through.
No smoke, no fear, no sound
of sirens in the distance, nor
need to hurry in or out.

The Pale Man's Eyes Never Leave the Horizon

—Lake Champlain

When a wave rolls up out of nowhere,
  do not look down. It is my body
shifting under the surface.

  I will be there in the shallows
to hear the people of the woods
  warn you not to disturb me.

My eyes, the size of white perch,
  will roll back into their sockets
at the sound of your laughter.

  Whenever your children come to the shore
aching to disappear into my calm lake,
  I will grab them by their ankles,

draw them into the deep water
  with their last breaths still captive
in their lungs. For each beating heart

  I devour, each of your barges
full of tree trunks I sink, you
  will cry a slow prayer toward

the dying light. There is no lesson
  in this pain for you, no
road you can build long enough

to escape my reach, the teeth
I sharpen each night, waiting
        for the crunch of bones you are.

Dusk, Meditation

...like oysters observing the sun through the water,
and thinking that thick water the thinnest of air.
                    —Melville

Sometimes the truth hides in the wide open
        of a shorn cane field, and no matter how you stare

its lines will refuse to define themselves. They'll pulse
        in the dull breeze, and spread like ribbon snakes

across furrows in the dirt until the whole ground
        blends and furls in waves. Squint all you want,

or close the distance on foot. What's there to see
        won't shine any brighter. Open yourself

to the field's expanse like a shell in salt water.
        Purge your questions before they pearl.

Augury

—Queen Bess Island

Pelicans glide on wind currents,
                                    infinities of loops,
long sweeps over the Gulf,
                    short passes near their nests.
The island below them
                        rings a ghost of itself,
washes out with every heavy wind,
                                            each wave
pushed through by storms.
                                    Two birds in air
for each one on shore,
                        in constant rhythm.
The cadence of their lives
                    tells stories
in flattened shore grass, single eggs in sand—

movement and birth and loss.

                But what should they know
of erosion?   Togetherness?
            Space?   More water around them
with fewer fish to eat?   And when a barge
            full of dredged silt   beaches itself
onto their sand to fill in the island's
            shadows, how long will it take
to settle all flight?

New Beach, Elmer's Island

—Caminada Headlands, 2018

Before they brought this beach back
    with barge after barge of sand

scraped out of the Mississippi's delta,
    the island had melted to a thin strip

of grass where waves broke hard
    on their way to chew mainland coast.

No headland buffer to slow down
    the Gulf's salt water, no room to walk,

nowhere for cranes to nest—this place
    was a hyperlapse of loss, a door

not so much unlocked as off its hinges
    and left to rot away. Now, though,

acres of shore sprawl against the Gulf,
    full of shore birds. Tall dunes

ready the island for the water's hot rise,
    storms sure to come. One island

cannot stop the sinking inland,
    or put back cemeteries and roadways

washed away by tide, but it can
    buy us time. And all time is hope.

Beached Whale, Terrebonne Parish, 2016

Hard to imagine what drew the young
     bull sperm inland through Sister Lake

south of Dularge. No squid to chase toward the beach,
     no pod to follow into the cove, only shallow,

slow water and sand to hold its weight. I'd love
     to believe something in the line of trees along

the coast stoked its primal heart. How golden
     it would be if the whale's old kin walked past

trees like ours into their first salt water. So much
     better to hold that dream than know the whale

swam in, dizzy from the water's heat, drunk
     on bacteria, or gobs of loose oil, unwilling to accept

the gift of open Gulf and long, deep breaths.

Marsh Horses

On the way to drop bags of oyster shells
      into the water near Montegut
         to seed a new barrier

against the water's need, you'll see
      small islands held together
         by marsh grass rising

out of the lake, ghosts
      of a full coastline reaching
         out into the open pass.

Here and there, herds
      of marsh horses toe
         along the waterline,

heads down, nosing new grass
      growing at the islands' edges.
         They've learned to swim

from mass to mass for fresh growth,
      step gingerly on soft ground
         to stay upright.

Nothing about these animals
      belongs on so little land,
         but here they'll be, alive.

La Lechuza

Not the volume so much
            as the anger in her screeches
that causes all the lights in the car
            to blink and go out. Even a short squawk
will blister your ears. Her pain will fester
            inside your head, unhealed,
until you find yourself one day
            polishing the skull of a squirrel
you found in your front yard, setting it
            gently in a safe place
to horde like a family jewel. From the moment
            you hear her cry, only dead things
will hold beauty for you. At some point
            during every conversation you have
with a neighbor, or mailman, or lover,
            their flesh will melt away. You will
want to follow their bones home.
            This cannot be helped
any more than the owl's cry can be unheard.
            Tie seven knots in twine
to wear around your neck if you'd like.
            It might buy you some time to hold
the living close. It might even turn
            their blood red again on your hands.

Pecan Grove with Body Farm

Scrub brush sprawled and dead vines
along the edge of the trees, and bones

lying in fresh dirt. What would a deer
need to bring it here? Nothing green

to eat, no smell of new grass or
water to draw it into this clearing.

It chews a rib bone as quietly
as it can, skittish but not ready

to leave. I'm sure it would rather
crack pecan shells in its teeth

for soft meat, but it has this grave
all to itself, and more bones around its feet.

The White Alligator

—for Emma

The white alligator at the zoo
rests his head on top the water
with only his blue eyes showing.

He hangs his body straight down
like any of us would, floating,

does not miss the sun
burning his pale skin, the pull
of mud in cold weather.

He does not fret for need.
I'm sure when his lids nictate shut,

he dreams of water-green hide
and a deer's total suppliance
nosing water from the bank's edge.

What more could his slow smile want?

City of Nature

—Kota Ezawa, 2011

Wind noise and water flow,
          bird calls,   violins,

hawks gliding   on   currents,
          squirrels in trees,   rain drops

falling from leaves,   insect screech,
          banjo,   mountain peaks,

river bank to ocean tide,
          shark fin,   sunset,

mist through sky,   repeat—
          nature through the prism

of movie sound: *Deliverance,*
          Twin Peaks, First Blood, Jaws.

Black Rush

My daughter notices it first,
      a black spot in the marsh grass.
The more we stare into it, the more
      it glides back and forth along the bank.
She watches the darkness without
      fear, her eyes focused beyond
the exposed roots at the water line.

I tell her a story my father told us
      about a shadow in the marsh
that could see inside anyone it came across.
      The shadow could read a person's
eyes for meanness, or for a kind lift,
      before two breaths were taken.
It knew you, even if you didn't.

If you held anything other than yourself
      dear, even a bird dog or doll,
the shadow blew across your face
      like winter breeze, took all moisture
from the air. If, though, you hid grudges
      or brokenness in your chest,
it became a black bear to claw you in half.

The whole while, she eyes the black rush,
      knows it isn't coming any closer,
can't cross water to join us in our boat.
      Its shimmer in the gold reeds
is no harbinger for her, not as long as the sun
      shines on our shoulders. It's a long time to night,
she says, and in the dark, black isn't black anymore.

Memory: Bats

My grandparents kept their freezer
　　　in an outbuilding behind the house
　　　　　so its compressor wouldn't make the kitchen

hotter than it had to be on summer days.
　　　I hated being sent out there
　　　　　to fetch a jar of something

or a broom left propped
　　　against the shed's doorframe.
　　　　　I thought the air in the room

was dead from being closed up.
　　　And the structure always
　　　　　scratched and moaned

with every step. Once,
　　　in late fall, I was sent out there
　　　　　to get ice cream after supper,

and as soon as I touched the freezer's handle,
　　　the tar wall behind it rippled.
　　　　　I ran inside to tell my uncle

because I knew he'd believe
　　　I wasn't too lazy to carry dessert,
　　　　　brought him back out with me

carrying his bulleye.
　　　The second we laid hands
　　　　　on the freezer's lid, the wall

woke, and we both jumped back.
       Uncle held the lamp up
              but didn't light it right away.

I'm pretty sure he thought
       we'd found a porthole to some place
              he did not want to go.

When finally he clicked his headlamp on,
       we saw the whole, living wall filled
              with bats tucked in like books on a shelf.

They held each other close, blinked their eyes
       against the harsh light as if the plague
              of morning had come upon them early.

Death Comes to the Banquet Table, ca. 1630-40

—oil on canvas, Giovanni Martinelli,
New Orleans Museum of Art

The last grain of sand drops
    into the bottom of the glass

and it simply does not matter
    that dessert has barely suffered

touch. This moment has not been
    chosen by any rubric

of convenience. Death does not
    sway choices until its invitation

is welcomed. And no degree
    of shock, no finger point,

no quick leap to the end of the table
    can alter its mission. Imagine

how that plum would have felt
    bursting on your palate.

Savor your idea of sweet, sweet
    peach for the rest of time.

Or stand in the shadows, unimpressed,
    if you wish. Only so many grains

of sand exist, and Death's hour glass
    is smaller than anyone cares to admit.

Goujon

—after Mai Der Vang's "Phantom Talker"

The old men will tell you, I am
the dark thing with gaping mouth

waiting deep in the silt
under still waters.

You dream of meals
my thick body would yield.

Spread out your poles,
hooks, corks, frozen shrimp.

Nothing in your tackle box
can pull me from this mud.

My patience is black
as time itself.

And even if you tied
the shiniest of spinners

near your hook to call me out,
you have no line that would pass my test.

Rolled Over into Waves

—White River, 1915

It had to be something the farmer did,
      they thought, when all the catfish
               disappeared and the water
on the river went choppy with crests
      every evening about sundown.

But then there were the bellows
      like a hurt mule when nobody
               for miles could have bought
or fed an animal like that, and to what end
      up against the water like they were.

Wind came and never left that summer,
      and all the kids started singing songs
               about a water elephant
rolling around under the river's surface
      big as two tractors and hungry

as dirt with no seed, thirsty as August
      without a drop of rain.
               Folks still fished,
though faith was a piss-poor bait
      and an even sorrier supper.

Voucher

When there's a ferry ride
over to Algiers for breakfast,
    flat water and high sun,

I'm never quite sure
    how to approach

How's it going?

There's always "Pretty good,"

but sometimes I
    have to think of my oldest

son, taller than I am and already
driving, his brother much better
at getting away with things
    than I ever was,
my daughter, whose every particle
    keeps my mother's memory
present.
        And then my wife's
smile when the warm coffee mug
    touches her hands each day.

It makes me think
    of stories my father
only told once:

Like in 1933, at six, how he had to
    walk downtown one day with a voucher
stuffed in his pocket that would get his family
    one cooked goose, or two live.

He couldn't carry both birds
      back home, so took off his belt,
looped it around the largest goose's neck,
      tucked the other under his arm,
and headed off. He said he sang
      church songs to keep the small
goose from squirming loose, let
      the big goose walk them home.

He said the next two weeks were
           pretty good

      getting something other than
rice every meal. And it was

really special his folks let him
      name those geese.

Traiteuse

Always a fever
      the wild kicking of legs
and tears to tend.

Her soft prayers
      fill the room to overflowing.

No gift required to buy her willow bark,
fig sap,
           le sureau to calm all chills,

she only needs an invitation, a dark room

and faith.
          Copper pots of water,
rosary beads, elderberry tea—

it all gives way to her song,
      the hope that all things
pass   except the caring,

and all trials are doorways

      to grace.

Memory: Touch

Only parts of us will ever touch the parts of others.
—*Marilyn Monroe*

I think of my children's hair, wet
　　　with fever, the small of my wife's back
　　　　　after a bath, my father's forehead

when he's fallen and cut himself,
　　　my mother's shoulders whenever
　　　　　my head was too heavy

to hold up on my own,
　　　my brother's hands
　　　　　work-hard and tan,

the forearms of strangers
　　　sharing peace at Mass,
　　　　　the chests of friends

pressed against my own
　　　after a long absence,
　　　　　Santa's lap,

and others I cannot touch
　　　but feel nonetheless,
　　　　　or would touch

given the chance, like
　　　the midsection of any tall
　　　　　man wearing a long coat

walking toward me on the sidewalk,

just for fear he might be
     three kids, one on top the other.

St. Lucy Led to Her Martyrdom

—Bernardino Fungai, circa 1490

This scene began with a simple *NO*:

St. Lucy refused to lose her mother
     to a disease of the blood,
          so turned to St. Agatha in a dream.

She refused to horde her family's riches
     through life and into the tomb,
          so released them to ease suffering.

She refused a rich man's hand
     and so utterly angered him
          he denounced her to the Governor.

She refused Paschasius's demand
     that she burn an offering for the emperor,
          so he ordered her defiled.

She refused to go with the guards
     when they came to bring her to the brothel,
          so they tried to drag her off.

She refused to move one inch,
     so they hitched her to oxen
          that pulled until their train broke.

When St. Lucy refused to *be* moved,
     the guards piled wood at her feet
          and set it ablaze.

She refused to burn,
     so stood there calmly gazing at the hillside,
       until the flames died down.

The guards refused to let this pass,
     so stuck a sword halfway to its hilt
       into St. Lucy's back.

Even then, she refused to bend a knee,
     so here we are, communion wafer
       poised in air awaiting grace,

oxen sprawled out everywhere
     in the grass,
          exhausted.

Littoral

*It may be the Wild Man of the Woods is but a ghost
of the wild man within.*
              —*Molly Gloss*, Wild Life

In the space between water's edge
        and forest, the shoreline blooms
                with thimbleberry and clover—

sunlight, mist off reeds, and my back
        flat against the dew. Everything here
                provides. The breeze pushes

toward morning. The lake reminds
        in waves how easy fish
                would offer themselves to line.

Such a short walk for wood
        to grow the fire, so little work
                to get from here to another

day, more meals, more moonlight,
        stars against open sky.
                And only in sleep

will the tickle of eyes
        coming from the trees
                admit itself, the family

of movement just out of view
        reminding me of body heat
                and want, things the day

has no need to list, but the night,
     with so much room between its trees,
          calls back home in soft voice.

Stink

—Henderson Swamp

The swamp smells heavy
        like a soul tethered to the heat
dripping down every window.

                It slaps the glass with hairy arms,
leaves big prints along the basin's shore,
        berry scat at the base of cypress trees.

Easy to hit that smell and know
                it's been left by something old
and large as the trees themselves,

        something dark at its core,
                always moving
from home to home, lonely

        as the moon against black sky.
Can you breathe and not hear
                its claws scraping down

                        rusted metal?
Can you breathe and not
        lock all doors?

Sometimes the Alligator Gets to Write the Ending

My daughter has been watching the news
    every night this week, anxious for word

on the soccer team trapped in a cave in Thailand.
    Every newscast parses like a cliffhanger

for her, each night mixing sorrow and fear
    with a little hope: one night divers

find the team and swim back to let us know
    the boys are all alive, but hungry and cold;

the next, four boys are pulled out of the caves
    by guide wires, the rest left behind for another

day; then delays and worries of more water
    pouring in to drown the remaining before divers

can swim back to drag them free. The next night,
    domestic news of violence and murder

and political kerfuffle preempts the cave report,
    and my daughter is left to fret her own ending—

What if the rains come? What if the older boys
    are too big to fit through tight passages?

What if one of them kicks the wrong rock,
    and the whole thing caves in?

She's seen enough of the news now to know
    it isn't a chapter book rumbling downhill

toward a happy ending, or a fable holding its lesson
     safe until we're ready for it. In this tale,

the alligator is not compelled to carry the opossum
     safely to the other side of the bayou.

Sometimes You Get the Bull, Sometimes

—Angola Prison Rodeo, 2013
Photograph by Chandra McCormick

There's got to be a moment
    when the inmate clown

wants the bull to stomp him out,
    that long second when the dust

kicked up from the bull's charge
    rises toward heaven

and people in the stands
    hold all the air in their lungs,

that hard pause when it's not a life
    passing through the eye

of your mind's needle, but the sweet
    nothing of a day's real end.

Tomorrow holds more work in the field,
    more slop on metal trays for supper,

more time in lockdown playing chess
    through the bars of your cell, or

reading by whatever light makes it through
    the chain link fence outside your cage.

And who wouldn't think about that hard ground
    pressing into their spine, how

one quick punch from the bull's forelegs
     would push them straight into deep, deep

earth, no doctor needed, no crying to do, no
     way to hold a spade come morning?

Q&A

—for Thomas White

You'd probably chuckle to know I pass
your grave every morning bringing my kids
to school. They've asked all the questions
their teachers have told them to ask,
and I've answered as best I could:

Did he want to die?
                        Probably, but not
that night, and not in his parents' house.

How did it happen?
                        From the beginning?
Coltrane, Hendrix, the dude from Blind Melon.
They were all beautiful to him. Release.
A slowing of heart. Sleep. Stop.

What was it like?
                        He always said
it was like swimming in honey.

*Why would he do something that made him
sick every time he did it?*
                        The other side
of sickness or pain is heaven, and that
lasts much longer than it takes
to empty your stomach.

Do you miss him?
                     I miss the way his pick hand
moved so casually over the strings of his bass,
how perfectly his thumb glided
down the neck of his guitar. His
potato rolls, the glaze he made for pastries.

Why couldn't you stop him?
                     I held him
like a brother, threw him against the wall
by his collar like a parent, set him free
to make his own choice like God does.
That river only flows downhill.

What do you remember most about the last time you saw him?

This one I always have trouble answering out loud,
how your stubble felt like needles on my cheek.

Owl- and Wolf-Infested Lands

—after Bachelin

Always an angry wind. Sky
like smeared ink. Marsh grass

        bent away as salt water

creeps in through the canal. Cypress
knees poked up

along the path, no trees alive
      before the horizon
line. Our hearts, always
left
        napping back at camp, unwilling

      to leave the glow of bed, dreams
      of moon, flowers' soft
touch:
        morning, with cream

for coffee, eggs, open flame
      to heat cast iron, butter sizzle.

Water chokes everything here, hungry
for roots, skin, loose threads

      hanging from
      days' work, days'

          heat

that settles all wind, and voice. This night,

though,

> with its dank stars, its
> greasy air, sharp reeds no one can
touch. An endless winter
>> route

which has never led anyone anywhere.

Like Asin at the Edge of the Woods

What if my daughter took two steps
    too many into the river, lost
her balance on slick rock?

It would not matter
    there's no undertow,
not with catfish
    or copperheads pressing
bellies to the mottled bottom.

And even if the water had no
    interest in taking her,
the forest surely would

with its momma bear nosing
    our tent skirt before dawn,
its tar shacks cooking meth up the hill,

so much claw and tooth and black
    to disappear any of us
quick, eat the muscle off our bones.

Nearly enough
    to muffle the sounds of laughter
glowing from inside these trees,

or hide the outline of a girl
against the woods' dark trunks.

La Llorona Rests Her Feet in the Creek

The mountain lions always come to me
      in pairs at night, heads low,
            with ears peeled back, contrite.

They hear their own mothers
      tucked away in my screams,
            so walk the banks with me

as penance. I envy the satisfaction they feel
      after they've eaten. Their stomachs
            hang low to ground,

and their eyes close slower each blink.
      Air rumbles inside their ribs.
            Blood dries on their pelts.

I pray for time to pass like this for me,
      for my heart to calm its fire,
            this creek to wash my wounds clean.

There Is No Train but the Tracks Will Lead You There

—Honey Island

No need
               for maps or guides to find
the swamp's heart. Everything that touches
                 this mud leaves its own prints
to follow—eagles, nutria, black bear, gators—
                all claws to mark your way.
Trust your own nose to tell you
                   what smells
should not be followed. If you see gray fur
                      caught on a palmetto frond,
          or count four toes on any webbed tracks,
                   find the sun in the sky
               right away. West of dead center
                   means
         you've run out of time. Move
      in the direction any line on your palm
leads. Do not linger near shadows
                    or look straight
            into any yellow light.
                          Remember,
almost everything where you are can outrun you,
and what can't is drifting just below the surface
                of the water you just used
                  to cool your face.

There Is Wind

Yes, there is wind. And waves.
      For now, the ghosts of trees
and lines of reeds remain.
      The water, though, rises.
It warms. It rolls in like it
      always has. It eats away,
washes out, deposits sand
      somewhere else, somewhere
pelicans won't be able to use it.
      The water leaves whole islands
places where they will not
      protect our shore. The water
carries its salt into new grass
      and tree roots until whole maps
loosen, coastlines untie, until
      wind and waves curve
over the horizon in every direction,
      and only the shadows of clouds
break the water's surface.

In the Open Space of a Crawfish Pond

a whooping crane chick pecks its way
    through acres of shallow water,

bigger than you'd think and unmistakably
    new. Its parents bellow in the distance

to warn it of motors rumbling
    near the banks, or fishermen casting

from the reeds. Here now, and safe,
    it will grow tall on crawfish

before flying away to find a mate
    of its own. It's easy, now, to think

of this pond full of chicks
    in ten years, when months ago

there was only flat land and warm breeze.

Présage

I've had old people down the bayou
       tell me animals carry all the truth

I need to know. Any snake hanging
       from a tree means illness is on its way;

one swimming on top the water
       says someone will leave you soon;

cattle sprawled out on the ground
       open gates for a new storm;

a turtle staring at you before you notice it
       sees something bent in your soul;

blue herons alone in the marsh call
       for dead relatives, begging you to remember.

Should a cat drop a mole at your feet,
       though, you need to turn and run.

The News, Again

My daughter wants to know
what that whale is thinking

carrying its dead calf around
on its snout for seventeen days.

I tell her its pain is probably a lot
like ours. We all do the best we can

with it. She wants to know
if the whale thinks its calf

will come back to life
if she just keeps carrying it.

I tell my daughter we all hold on
to hope as long as we can. She asks

if the whale's hope is bigger
than ours because it's a whale.

I tell her all hope can swell
to fit our idea of God. She wants

to know if that hope dies, too,
if we don't take care of it.

I think of how my eyes always
well up at Mass when we sing

"grant us peace," and tell her
our souls give us hope that won't die,

but it can turn like milk to cheese
if we keep it in the wrong place too long.

Conflation

1.

Yesterday at the riverfront, the water
      rose so high a man washed
his socks from the rubble placed along the bank
      to guard the walking path. His socks
were filthy from slogging through the Quarter
      during the morning's flood. As hot
as it was, those socks must have felt
      divine on his feet, like a river of cool breeze
carrying him to his next shady spot. He did not
      rush the washing. He had no need
to leave any of the river behind.

2.

Two years ago, I got a call from my brother
      in the morning to let me know our father
had passed away. I was vacuuming at the time,
      getting the living room ready for Dad
to stay with us on the weekend like he'd done
      every week since our mother died.
I remember the sound of the vacuum's handle
      slapping the wood floor, how my knees
unhinged. I remember looking across the room
      at my father's green chair. The rest,
just a blur from then to now.

3.

Memory bears weight. No doubt. Riverfront,
      brother, father, flood, breeze,

living room. This load carries, want to or not.
       I could drop it, but it would need
picking up. I could wash it, but it would
       dirty itself again. Weight is a force
of being. Choice, just a pretty song.

Neighbor Tones

All a musician can do is to get closer to the sources of nature,
and so feel that he is in communion with the natural laws.
—John Coltrane

In Coltrane's circle, all tone
        shares a common ancestor.
The vibrations between F and F#
                wave in invitation. Tremolos
        whisper desire, not dispute,
and every pitch shares a bit of itself
                with its neighbor, like electrons
swapped during the intimacies of physics.

Even when scales cannot
        reconcile themselves geometrically,
we can choose to hear them
                together. We can transpose
        the culture of sound, make room
for the diminished and the supertonic.
                These connections yearn to be
made, even if our ears resist.

How much of ourselves
        do we leave with each other
taking the same seat on a bench, or
                grabbing the same spot on the handrail
        to pull our weight upstairs?
We share the breeze, the noise
                it carries. The space between us,
never empty, is full of us.

Jack B. Bedell is Professor of English and Coordinator of Creative Writing at Southeastern Louisiana University where he also edits *Louisiana Literature* and directs the Louisiana Literature Press. Jack's work has appeared in *Southern Review, Birmingham Poetry Review, Pidgeonholes, The Shore, Cotton Xenomorph, Okay Donkey, EcoTheo, The Hopper, Terrain, saltfront,* and other journals. His previous collections include *No Brother, This Storm* (Mercer University Press, 2018) and *Color All Maps New* (Mercer University Press, 2021). He served as Louisiana Poet Laureate, 2017-2019.